About the Author

The author, Dr Aqib Shaick was born on 7th may 1972. Is an Indian national hails from Kerala state. A practicing Oncosurgeon at his native place. He is happily married to Dr Simmi, a Gynecologist. They have two daughters, Aasmi Aqib and Bismi Aqib.

THE MUSINGS OF STARS AND DUST

Dr Aqib Shaick

THE MUSINGS OF STARS AND DUST

Olympia Publishers
London

www.olympiapublishers.com
OLYMPIA PAPERBACK EDITION

Copyright © Dr AqibShaick 2024

The right of **Dr Aqib Shaick** to be identified as author of
this work has been asserted in accordance with sections 77 and 78 of
the Copyright, Designs and Patents Act 1988.

All Rights Reserved

No reproduction, copy or transmission of this publication
may be made without written permission.
No paragraph of this publication may be reproduced,
copied or transmitted save with the written permission of the publisher,
or in accordance with the provisions
of the Copyright Act 1956 (as amended).

Any person who commits any unauthorised act in relation to
this publication may be liable to criminal
prosecution and civil claims for damage.

A CIP catalogue record for this title is
available from the British Library.

ISBN: 978-1-83543-360-7
This is a work of fiction.
Names, characters, places and incidents originate from the writer's
imagination. Any resemblance to actual persons, living or dead, is
purely coincidental.

First Published in 2024

Olympia Publishers
Tallis House
2 Tallis Street
London
EC4Y 0AB

Printed in Great Britain

Dedication

I dedicate this book to my dear family.

Acknowledgements

Thank you to Ms Bismi Aqib, my younger daughter for helping me write this book.

GENIE IN THE BOTTLE

Wild creatures came to
Wet market, furtively came
With them deadly corona to
Wreak havoc to mankind.

What a mayhem it was like a
Wild elephant on the loose.
Who and how to tame the
Wild tusker was the query.

Mahouts of virology dug trapping pit
Marauding menace was felled in it
Made sketches of the contour
Managed to chain in lockdown.

Reined in with vaccine muzzle
Restive tusker was restrained, changed
Role from pandemic to endemic to
Rest as the 'elephant in the room'.

Musths of mutation strike randomly, the
Mellowed fellow breaks the shackles.
Milder are the harms as it loses stings at the
Mighty armour of acquired antibodies.

Corona was uncorked like someone

'Let the genie off the bottle'.
Corona the genie, a lurking danger
Lays in wait to pounce as it wishes.

WHO DID IT ?

Show me if there is one, make me
Hear at least for me to believe.
Sans seeing or hearing
Hard to believe his existence.

Had you heard the mumble
Heralding the seismic, shouldn't
Have got buried under the rubble. Heard it and
Hurried the creatures of the woods and fields.

Ultrasound uncovered your unborn.
Unwavering is your eardrum to the
Hush and hoot under and over the
Hearing range of your dumb head.

Our vibes are quite different
You will not sync with me.

Unseen was the fire that
Stealthily burnt your back.
Ultraviolet and infrared rays
Stay clear of your eyes.

Our wavelengths are different
We won't get along well.

Consciousness is the result of
Connection of neurons and there
Can't be a soul, you questioned my
Competence and conscience.

Lurking in the dark is the dark energy
Lavishly fill up the universe, infinitesimally
Less is the energy that you brought to
Light, still you pride in your smattering.

Laws of physics don't care about a
Creator, you scoff. but you ignore the
Chemistry behind matter.Mind it, physics
Labour on the goods delivered by chemistry.

Parrots' shades and the Showbiz of
Peacocks are accidents of evolution for you.
The final nail in the coffin not on me alone as
The creator, but on my creativity also.

Letters randomly fall and by stroke of
Luck literary masterpieces are born
Talent and wisdom have no role to play, I
Taunt and take the liberty to contradict.

I presented evidences galore, but
You looked the other way.
I am the "who" and I alone know the "why"
You are exploring only the "how"

LONE WOOD

Lone wood standing in the woods,
Long life is what I am blessed with, l
Sympathised on their plight when the
Short lived trees perished presenile.

Once a fruit tree, I was a shade tree too,
Fed many, provided shade and shelter, but
Fled the woods when they took wings,
Orphaned me in this orchard of life.

Still blooming, albeit not as before
Still intact is my canopy, though sparse.
No one is there to savour the fruits,
No one needs the cool canopy.

My value is reduced to a mere wood
Money will go to nominees
When I fall down for good, that's
What my only worth today.

Lucky are the short lived ones, who
Succumb soon after fulfilling their due.
Long life is not a blessing, but a matter of
Sympathy if lived longer than required

WE DON'T CROSS PATHS

Forests, hills, deserts, oceans,
Fresh water and water bodies
God gifted ecosystems,
Grazing lands for life.

Animals took to forest, water by
Aquatic creatures. The rest were
Allocated appropriately, never did the
Almighty anticipate encroachment.

Brachiating apes embarked on
Bipedalism and raced to civilization,
Built villages and townships
Breached the world order.

Wilds shrunk, animals were crammed
We roamed through the forest, but
Were blamed for straying into your land
Wondered when it was taken away.

Foraged through vegetations
Fed on fruits and vegetables, you
Faulted us for damaging crops, we
Failed to gather that was agriculture.

Strolled straight through the woods
Still blamed us for crossing the road, you
Wantonly cut paths across the woods,
We never crossed paths with you.

Nobody taught us that, whatever
Fenced are produce of cultivation, the
Path that cuts across the forest is road
And the wilds ceded to civilization.

THE TRAPPED SOUL

Wish to fly high in the sky
Seek to scale the Everest summit
Set my heart to roam around the universe
Way above the speed of light.

A whole universe inside an atom
Ardently wish to savour the splendid
Desirous to take a plunge
Deep into the Mariana trench.

Wish to caress the sun and to
Witness a supernova from it's backyard
Dive into a black hole and to get
Delivered from a white hole.

Umpteen obstacles to overcome
Unfortunately everything is bodily
Gravity to overpower, hunger and thirst to
Gain mastery over to name a few.

Got trapped in this body a
Good fifty years back, need to
Get out of this impeding body to
Get rid of these myriad hurdles.

Millions and billions are the
Marvels happening in the nature
Negligible is my life among these
Numerous wonderful events

Why should I worry about death as
Windows of many a wonder may open
When I leave this thwarting frame.
What's in store could be a cut above "life."

DIGGING OWN GRAVE

The breeze, the drizzle and
The balmy days have forsaken us forever.
Why have they deserted us so?
What on earth did cause this?

Torrent came and trampled down
The drizzle, while tempest blew the
Breeze away, balmy days were
Burnt away by the blistering heat.

Felled the woods, fuelled your gluttony
Filled the sky with smoke and gas
Furthered your fortune and ego
Furnace is what you made the planet

The heat of your haught awaken
The watergiant in the poles,
Thaw from slumber are the glaciers
The oceans swell, islands are guzzled.

Come what may, will achieve
Carbon neutral, you pledge
Won't go beyond a degree and a half
Which turned out to be a lot of hot air.

Can't take even a decimal more
Care to come out of the hole
Don't dig your own grave
Discretion is the need of the hour.

IT'S TIME FOR SOME CHARITY

Snatched the fruit of his
Sweat and toil, had
Square meal for you, while
Squarely denied any meal to him.

Evicted in the pretext of encroachment
Erected palatial bungalow.
Even stole his brainchild and
Empire was built over his skeleton.

Shoved his children into child labour,
Sent yours to five star schools.
Nipped his dream in bud and
Nurtured yours sturdy.

Earned an ailing body,
Acute abandonment and skype chats
Every now and then from the other shore.
At last that's your balance sheet.

"It's time for some charity", you surmised
Is charity a repentance to cheating, or
Is it a repayment to the deserving.
It's too late anyhow.

THE FOOL'S PARADISE

Wonder what will become of Gen Z?
Why they wantonly deny the almighty.

Scant regard to the holy book
Strutting the path to the inferno
Attaining heaven not in the agenda
Agnostics, atheists and the likes.

There in the days of yore, happily
Thrived our forefathers in the woods
Thirst and lust were doused at will
Teamed up and mauled down the hunger.

In came the saints, prophets and sanyasis
"Is this the way you endure the life?
Earthly life is ephemeral, try to attain
Eternal life up in the heaven".

"Where's the heaven?" Queried
The unenlightened curiously

"Up among the clouds"
Uttered the rudraksha clad
"Beyond seven skies", the
Bearded brazenly lied.

Everlasting youth awaits you there
Everything served in plenty
Perennial penetration of virgins galore
Palatial bungalow and rivers of beverage.

"Why the Gen Z is like this still?"
Wondered the sapient souls.
Pat came the answer
Plenty to ponder

Clouds are very much earthly, not
Celestial bodies mind it, couldn't
Capture a glimpse of the gods while
Cruising through the clouds.

Sky is not real, but an optical illusion
'Seven skies' a paranoia to say the least
Pinning the hope of heaven
Past the skies is nothing but stupidity.

Innumerable women and wine are
In our wish list, but the clairvoyant
In you failed miserably to foresee
The bucket list of our wishes.

The unlimited wifi, the HD channels,
The merc, the Rolls-Royce, the yacht
The pizza and the KFC are not
There in your offer.

Better rewrite the holy books or
Bless us with novel decoding
Leave us alone, you may
Live in your fool's paradise.

'BLIND' FAITH

Faith is in distress
Faint vision is the bother
Fainted out of fear
Faith is under care.

Medics mulled it over
Many a reason crossed their mind
Mindful of them will help to
Mend the vision.

"Curtain of superstition might have
Covered the cornea"

"Greed, the termite might have
Gnawed the sight nerve"

"Supple lens might have been
Smeared with selfishness"

"Might of ignorance might have
Malnourished the faith".

Science and science alone is the
Sole solution to this sickness
Faith needs to be rescued
From turning into 'blind' faith.

THE MARTYR

She started stalking me ever-

Since I started walking
Beautiful nightwalker
Bright and gleaming.

Ardently fell in love as she
Avidly watched over me
Decided to meet her as
Desire overhauled me.

Not yet felt her proximity, I lamented.
"Neither beautiful nor nice,
Nightwalker could be a devil" was some
Nerd's words of caution.

Hearsay could be lies
Hence I decided to
Send an undercover agent
Similar to a 'Trojan horse'.

Residing afar, so to
Reach her fired a rocket away
Revolving around and around
Reached cleverly near her.

"Bearhug" is her habit to
Bring about the end
Crushing the bones, so
Care to be taken when near.

'Vikram lander' was my Trojan
Weathered the virile embrace to
Touch down on her and
Tactfully released the 'Pragyan'.

Pitted against the odds, he
Steered clear of the umpteen
Pits of death trap and uncovered her
Secrets galore till his demise.

A martyr's end truly at
A moon day's culmination.

THE EXODUS

Flock of birds, "Probably
Fleeing their homeland", I presumed
Waylaid the curious me
"What happened?" I implored.

Who uprooted your perch?
Who grabbed your pastures?
Whose god prevailed over yours?
What policy decreed your exile?

We are on annual migration
Not on eternal exodus
Unlike you the unlucky.
None decreed our exile, We
Obey commands of nature alone.

No boundaries are big enough
No divisive laws are strong enough
Nothing can be a hindrance to us.
Undivided we move
Unity is our strength.

Greener pastures beckoning us
Food and fertilisation
What we are after

Withering winter forced us out
No one grabbed our land.

Spring will welcome back with all
Smiles and splendor
Adorned perches above
And purple carpet below.

Meandering journey we undertake
Many will not see the end
The weaker will drop down dead
The slothful will be preyed upon
The least we complain about
The Nature taking its course.

We don't have to jump the walls of division
The barricades of law doesn't push us back
We don't have to row to the shore of hope
We don't have to drown in the ocean of despair

'World is one family', but
You will erect boundary walls,
You will push back the immigrants and
You will 'stop the boats' too.

A STILL BIRTH

Religion, a dead horse
Rituals flogged and impregnated it
Miracles nourished the fetus, delivered
Myth, a stillborn baby.

None had seen the myth
Many have seen those who saw it
Plenty have heard about it too, Apostle
Tongues rendered life to the stillborn.

Makes space travel sans Oxygen
Makes wine out of water sans Chemistry
Completes surgeries sans Science
Continues to be an enigma sans evidence.

Defended by the disciples, though it
Defies science and even logic.
"Dreadful afterlife is what awaits the
Deniers" rave the disciples.

Myth gets hoisted on a pedestal of lies
Myth is no longer a dead baby.
" My myth is robust and alive
Your myth is the real stillborn".

THE MASTER BLASTER

To peep into the past
Pressed into action were
Few telescopes, Hubble,
The novel JWST and more.

The curious me also
Took a plunge, perplexed
By the sight beheld. Someone squats
Beside the barrel of singularity.

Ignites the barrel and disappears
From the realm of space-time.
A colossal blast follows
The creation happens.

Dust, smoke and energy
Emanate and disperse.
The dust of the then being
The me and you of now.

The fidgety fellow
Did it in a flash
Far below a week's task
Handed over the reins to evolution.

Stars, planets and the
Entire Universe, the living
And the non-living had to
Evolve from these very dusts.

Created with a blast
Sustains with several blasts
Will destroy with another blast
The master blaster.

Eternally remains elusive
Blasts away in his
Merry way cracking stars & supernovae
Flinging asteroids & comets.

Where does he reside?
Is he in the vast expanse or
Beyond the infinity,
The quest is on and on......

THE EMPTY NEST

Flung out with torn apart heart
Flew down to me like a sparrow
I took you under my wings
In my heart you nested.

Rowed out from the sea of
Sorrows in the vessel, my care.
My passionate embrace provided
The potion to heal your wounds.

Barely had the scars faded
You pleaded " The prince of my dream
Has arrived, let me gallop
On the horseback of my desire".

I opened the door
You flew out of the nest
Stole my heart and eloped
Never to be seen again.

I still keep the door ajar
Waiting at the threshold
Expecting a rare clandestine visit
As the nest is still empty

IT'S THE STAR'S TURN

It's our turn
For the star turn,
Baseless blames
Error filled extolls,
The source of light
We are throwing light
On many a glaring fact.

Brooded in to the cradle
Of heaven extravagantly
We little (big) stars predestined.
Perpetually on the run
From the moment we are born
Peace of mind is alien
Many an explosion
Keeps our heart beating.
Bite the dust in profusion
Dissipate to dust and smoke
In the cradle of sky
Nay, graveyard the sky.

Neither do we smile and wink
Nor watch over and smirk
We do not care about
Your deeds or fate

We, the ill-fated.

Your dead and dusted
Kin are not us dude
The long perished
Stars are what you behold.
Not reincarnations, satans or guides,
but, few curious constellations.

We burn away
The self-destructive way
To show you the way
To be the light of your life
It's our turn
For the star turn.

THE FLIRTERS

They come night after night
After she wished good night
Unsure whether she's aware
Or feigning to be unaware
Is my legitimate partner.

Must not be aware as they
Tickle, pinch, prick
and evade my grasp
While she's fast asleep
Fondle, fiddle, flirt
Until sun is out.

Some are after my blood
Pinch n prick with purpose
Suck blood for sustenance
Some barge blindly
Crawl, tickle and elope.

They come night after night
Out they fly from cabinet
Cupboard and kitchen
Creepy crawlers
And purring prickers.

TRUTH IN HIBERNATION

Truth was in hibernation
Extreme weather dwindling food
Had to weather
The dark winter
Truth is for all seasons so
Truth was in hibernation not
To be seen in the light

Faith vowed
Science seeked
To find him out

Faith was out
Of the block first
Intuition fuelled the pursuit
Met ignorance on the path
Guaranteed to guide forth
In the headwind
Of superstition found
Drifted away and away
Blanket of fear
Blinded it forever.

Science was slow to start
Rationale fuelled the pursuit

Met research on the way
Guaranteed to guide all the way
In the tailwind of evidence
Closed in on ever so close
Unveiled the blanket
Unearthed the truth.

Truth was in hibernation
Had to weather
The dark winter
As truth is not
A fair weather friend.

AGE IS JUST A NUMBER

Look at my skin

No wrinkles yet,
Look at my hair
So thick still.
Don't look at my age
Age is just a number.

The botox jabs
Have bolstered the cutis
The hair transplants
Planted back the youth
Threw me back in time.
I am an evergreen
Handsome debonair
Age is just a number.

Your shrinking brain quarrels
"why spared planting
memory you bald".

Your flirting heart flutters
In the see-saw of desire,
Clogged coranaries are
Waiting to shut shop.

Caught up with wear and tear
Your joints just can't
Catch up with mind's gallop
Be truthful to your tardiness.

Curtain of cataract is about
To fall down in front
of your presbyopic passion,
Gropes in the dark is
The illusion of youth.

The evening siren
Blares at the hepatic factory
About to call it a day
Synthesis will soon cease.

You look back finally to
Stare in disbelief the
space-time encroachment
By the worthy youth.
The tide of time
Throws you forth
Bangs the head on the
Boulder of reality
Back to sanity you senile.

THE BOY NEXT DOOR

Once part of my schemes but,
Shown the door in
The days of yore,
Settled in the neighbourhood as
The boy next door.

Peep through the window in
The shades of dark,
Attractive you are but
Annoyance to me.

Stir up unrest in my
Blue eyed girl
Prowl round and round
Wielding the magic wand
Lure her you lunar
Turn her lunatic.

Nearer you are aroused
Waves of eroticism,
Farther you are
Bangs her head on
The shore of despair.

Attractive you are but

Annoyance to me
Once part of my schemes but
Shown the door in
The days of yore.

BURNING ISSUE

Surplus than a
Square meal. A
Source of waste.
Starvation. A
Burning issue for
Some. Disposal, a
Burning issue for
Some others.

Expectation in excess of
Essentials generates
Extra. Extra, a
Burning issue for the
Elites. Privation, a
Burning issue for the poor.

Surplus and extra, a
Burning issue for the
Society at large.

Scavengers devour to
Survive on the surplus and
Settle the issue, but
Setup the issue are
The flightless vultures, looting

The broad daylight,
Set aflame the extra at
Sundown. Blazing and burning
Smouldering and smoke,
The perilous issue.

Burning desire of a few
Brings about a
Burning issue for many, Yes
The issue is burning still.

GHOST IN THE SKY

Died an untimely death with
Unfulfilled dreams brewing still.
Resurrected from ashes
Devours anything in your grasp
Ghost in the sky with insatiable
Yearning of unfulfilled dreams.

Shrunken star in an ever
Expanding universe.
Wonder, why you are so black even after feasting on the
Brightest of stars.
Snares out shooting stars
For pickle in the dish.
Grapples gropes gives up
Being fastest is of no avail
Light can't sneak
Out of your jail.
Ghost in the sky with
Insatiable yearning of unfulfilled dreams.

Wonder what would have been
The fate of we eight
Had it not been for
Our dad's power
Sun the saviour.

Christened Sagittarius A*
Ghost in the milky way with
Insatiable yearning of unfulfilled dreams.